THE MOTHERHOOD PROJECT

MONOLOGUES AND REFLECTIONS ON MOTHERHOOD

Kalhan Barath E.V. Crowe **Juno Dawson**
Suhayla El-Bushra **Jodi Gray** Hannah Khalil
Katherine Kotz Morgan Lloyd Malcolm **Siggi Mwasote**
Irenosen Okojie **Anya Reiss** Naomi Sheldon
Lemn Sissay Athena Stevens **Joelle Taylor**

NICK HERN BOOKS
London
www.nickhernbooks.co.uk

A Nick Hern Book

The Motherhood Project first published in Great Britain in 2021 as a paperback original by Nick Hern Books Limited, The Glasshouse, 49a Goldhawk Road, London W12 8QP

Introduction copyright © 2021 Katherine Kotz. Individual works copyright © 2021 Hannah Khalil, Morgan Lloyd Malcolm, Suhayla El-Bushra Ltd, Jodi Gray, Naomi Sheldon, Katherine Kotz, Anya Reiss, E.V. Crowe, Irenosen Okojie (see additional copyright notice on p. 62), Juno Dawson, Joelle Taylor, Siggi Mwasote, Athena Stevens, Kalhan Barath, Lemn Sissay

The authors have asserted their moral rights

Cover image by Ruby Lloyd-Burman

Designed and typeset by Nick Hern Books, London
Printed in the UK by Mimeo Ltd, Huntingdon, Cambridgeshire PE29 6XX

A CIP catalogue record for this book is available from the British Library

ISBN 978 1 83904 008 5

Contents

Introduction
Katherine Kotz

I set up *The Motherhood Project* as a way of bringing artists together to respond to the needs of the pandemic. Inspired by the groundswell of activism in 2020, and particularly the Black Lives Matter movement, I had been reading about the rise in calls to the domestic-violence charity Refuge, and I wanted to coordinate an artistic collaboration that would both raise money and send out a public message of solidarity to anyone feeling invisible and unsafe in lockdown.

Creatively, I was keen to engage with new writing on the topic of motherhood because I was pregnant and grappling with my own preconceptions about what lay ahead. I'd always considered motherhood to be quite a hard sell. Bearing in mind that it's 2021 and women are still performing eighty per cent of unpaid care responsibilities, we could be forgiven for being a little hesitant about leaping open-armed into family life. In my experience, women don't tend to talk very openly about motherhood for fear of offending one another, or seeming selfish or inadequate in some way. As a society we're still quite quick to attach labels to women if they choose not to have children – we want to know why.

This collection is an attempt to dig into the issue and engage with a cross-section of different perspectives. I had the idea to mix real-life reflections with dramatic pieces and produce them in a fairly rudimentary way to raise money for Refuge. One by one, playwrights and authors I admired agreed to contribute something and the line-up grew ever more exciting and varied. A brilliant production company called Drift Studio agreed to help me produce the films, and waived their fee to shoot and edit them – an extraordinarily kind act which meant we could be far more ambitious on an extremely limited budget.

As lockdowns came and went, the project steadily grew. Fifteen short films were made and edited, and a streaming partner found in Battersea Arts Centre. A magnificent effort on everyone's part.

My baby was born when we were halfway through creating the films. I can confidently tell you that it's incredibly hard to juggle working with being a new mum, not least because the sleep deprivation turns you into a monosyllabic yeti for whom 'spare time' amounts to doing some mental arithmetic of your baby's bowel movements while you hunt around the kitchen for old bits of toast. As I write this, my six-month-old is beaming at me as he massages banana into the sleeve of my once-favourite shirt, a fitting end to this fading relic from my past life.

The pieces you're about to read are not sequential or thematically linked. It was my intention to gather a wide range of writing on the subject. I hope this collection forms part of a wider conversation about our attitudes to women and motherhood and how they could be reimagined.

Acknowledgements

Special thanks to Ali White, Crusoe Weston, Magda Koc, Jake Strutt, Natasha Patel, Laura Wyatt O'Keefe, Francesca Moody, Hannah Philp, Hannah Peaker, Jo Langdon, Ash Parker, Chloé Nelkin Consulting, Nick Hern Books and Battersea Arts Centre.

The Motherhood Project was generously supported by Drift Studio, Lucian Msamati, Jo Rado, Lis & Russell Strutt, Magda Koc, Charlie Burman, Julie Lloyd, Arndt Peterhansel, Michas Kotz, Alice Tennant, Zosia Williams, Lucy Harding, Soph Quin, Sue Bramwell Smith, Mysia Koc, Lesley Wood, Sonia Cala-Lesina, Gabriela Cala-Lesina, Barbara Cala-Lesina, John Foster, Pauline Marsden, Tom Spencer, Trevor Strutt, Licia Kotz, Lou Stephens, Harriet Phillips, Hannah Hooper, Carda Best, Alison Harper, Caroline Hearst, Cicely Taylor.

SUITED

Hannah Khalil

Performed by Emmanuella Cole
Directed by Caroline Byrne

Director of Photography and Editor Crusoe Weston
Sound Designer Sinéad Diskin
Camera Assistant Alex Mead
Thanks to Robin Allen

You wouldn't have understood before.

(*A beat.*)

You only bleed for a few days. Weeks. Months. That toe-curling pain passes. Eventually. It's natural. Normal. The pain. The bleeding is normal. The hair falling out is normal. The hair on your boobs is normal. Those freckles are normal. That tiredness is normal.

Normal.

It's normal not to want to be touched.

Normal not to want to be sucked or held.

Normal.

(*A beat.*)

The stretch marks don't go though. You're stuck with those.

(*A beat.*)

You wouldn't have understood before.

(*A beat.*)

Enjoy it now, this age passes so quickly. Make sure you hold yourself when you go to the toilet so the stitches don't burst. Cabbage leaves help. Put your pads in the freezer. Try not to worry.

(*A beat.*)

She's very small. He's very big. Breast is best. Get her on the bottle as soon as you can.

Don't wake the baby to feed her. Feed him every three hours.

Sleep when the baby sleeps.

I hope he's sleeping through.

Remember when you were worried about the birth?

You wouldn't have understood before.

(*A beat.*)

Hold him like this. This. This. This.

Not like that.

Try not to worry

(*A beat.*)

The days pass slowly but the years go quickly. Enjoy this age.
It's going to fly by. Get up every day. Get dressed. Go out. Take
him swimming. To baby massage. Monkey music. Baby yoga.
Fit baby to your routine. Bring her into the office. Remind them
you're still alive. Visit friends. Go on holiday. It's easy when
they're that age. It's cheap when they're that age. Enjoy it now,
this age passes so quickly.

(*A beat*.)

Once it's come out you can't imagine anything going up there
again. But it will. Wear a bra or you'll get milk everywhere. Not
sexy. Pretend you want to. That you don't mind everyone
owning all the bits of you, touching bits of you, holding bits of
you, sucking bits of you - that no bits of you are yours any
more. Nothing is private. Yours. Get used to that.

(*A beat*.)

Don't hate your body. It may look different but think about the
wonderful thing it did. Think about the fact it made a baby – a
miracle – and you bought it into the world. Of course you don't
look the same. Don't feel the same. Because everything is
different – changed – forever.

(*A beat*.)

A part of you is outside your body and walking around and
nothing will ever be the same again.

(*A beat*.)

Get used to it. Enjoy it. Try to.

You wouldn't have understood before.

(*End*.)

INSIDE ME

Morgan Lloyd Malcolm

Performed by Jenni Maitland
Directed by Maria Aberg

Director of Photography and Editor   Ali White
Camera Assistant   Max Quinton

She is sitting down on the bed in front of me as I stand. And she's like.

'This will feel a bit weird as I'm down here and you're up there but if you can just stand with your legs apart and relax a moment and I'll just…'

She starts to root about down there and.

'Let me just try and find the best way in as I'm doing it upside down from normal.' And she's got a finger in. Then she says.

'Now just shuffle your feet together a little. I know you can't get completely together as my hand is there but… there that's it, lovely. Now I want you to lift your pelvic floor for me so I can just have a feel of what you're doing.'

And I do something. I don't know what I'm doing to be honest but I give it a try. And she's like.

'Okay that's good'

Is it? Okay great, I'm thinking. I'll try and replicate.

And she says.

'Okay so you're managing to do it both at the front and back but I now want you to think of your vagina as a compass. With your north, south, east and west. And try and engage all sides. Or like purse strings. Pull it all together.'

I've got to pull it together. Yes I do. Pull it together.

She's talking to me quite seriously whilst also having a finger up me. Like she's got her digit completely inside me and we're having this chat. I find it very hard to maintain eye contact. I keep shutting my eyes so that it seems like I'm concentrating on the purse strings but really it's because I can't look her in the eye while I try to grip her finger with my vaj. And shutting my eyes is risky because I'm so fucking tired I feel like I could honestly fall asleep right now standing up with her inside me.

This is so fucking surreal.
She does this every day with so many women.
To help us all stop pissing in our pants when we sneeze or laugh. She's a fucking hero.

Also. And I feel like I need to put a 'too much information' warning on the next bit but it's probable that ship has sailed already. So…

I can smell myself.

Like. I basically get a waft. So she must have too. And it mortifies me because no matter how much feminist literature and activist freedom chat I've listened to I have had it deeply ingrained in me since childhood that my vagina is smelly and I need to do something about it. I had obviously showered this morning but the journey here and the Tena Lady and the slightly stressful school run obviously means I will have ended up with some kind of something going on down there and now I can smell it. I mean it's not unpleasant to me but to Danny Wilcox in Year 8 it's fucking disgusting and that's all I can think of. This poor woman is smelling my stinky vaj. When she's down the pub with her doctor friends is she going to be all like 'Fucking hell this WOMAN today. She has SUCH A PROBLEM VAGINA. It STANK.'

Isn't that so fucked up that this is what I'm worrying about? Right now? In this moment while this woman is trying to help me fix my body so that my everyday existence can be happier, can be less uncomfortable. Normal.

Well whatever I did whilst dealing with these thoughts, clearly was good because she was delighted with my squeeze. And then she says.

'Now you need to make sure you're engaging your tummy muscle and breathing. Let's try the lift on the breath out and afterwards keep holding and whatever you do keep breathing.'

Keep breathing, keep breathing. Yes. I must. Keep breathing.

It's a funny thing adulthood isn't it? Because when you were a kid you imagined it all in chunks of – Get job, get partner, get married, get kids, get house, get old, die. You don't imagine the minutiae. You don't imagine the small little fucking insane events that make up all those chunks. You don't imagine you'll spend Thursday mornings every six to eight weeks chatting about your vagina with someone who has their finger actually in it.

Also – you don't imagine that doing something like this will feel like a break. I may as well have been going to a spa the way I left the house this morning. Genuinely the last time I did something like this for myself was when I got two fillings and I practically had a snooze in the dentist's chair.

'Let me just show you another way to do this.'

She says withdrawing from me and removing her gloves. I catch a brief look at her finger and it's gloopy and wet and I panic thinking 'OH FUCK THAT'S MY HUSBAND'S SPERM FROM LAST NIGHT' but then I remember she used KY Jelly and I calm the fuck down.

'Just perch your bum on the edge of the bed and rest your elbows on your knees and engage your lower back so scoot your pelvis under a bit and make sure your back is straight that's it. Now do the same, draw your belly button up about ten per cent...'

Ten per cent of what? Of WHAT? I'm suddenly wondering if I'm even able to comprehend the details of all this. I barely understand what my vagina is doing when it's doing it. Whatever it is. I pull my tummy in and hope that's ten per cent.

'Not quite.'

Well no! Obviously! I've no idea what I'm doing! I've not got a single clue what I'm doing! What am I doing?! WHAT AM I DOING??!

She's very sweet to me to be honest. She sits me up and lets me just. Just let it out. Just let it all out. And she gives me a tissue and she suggests that maybe instead of doing the normal exercises we just have a chat and the kindness of this just makes me sob harder and harder and everything comes out. Everything about the last few years. She gets it all. She just sits there listening as I tell her about my first and all the hopes I had for his birth and his babyhood and how it all went wrong and how hopeless I felt for months. MONTHS. And no one really knew just how hopeless because you can't stop. And then it was just getting through it and surviving it and then trying to make it all feel like fun and how you hoped it would be before he came. And then number two happened and my body wasn't ready. I hadn't done the work, you know? I hadn't done enough so it felt like I was taking my car on a long-distance trip before I'd given it a service. And so what hope did it have? Really? And even though the birth was better the recovery was impossible because I had two of them now and they both needed such different things. And of course I'm grateful. Of course I am. Of course. But truly these physio appointments were the first real thing I'd done for my body since and it just feels like it's too little too late.

It's like when my boy smashed his face open at the playground and someone appeared next to me with a tiny plaster and everyone laughed because fucking hell. His whole face needed a plaster.

And honestly, honestly the exhaustion, *the exhaustion*. I am just too tired to do anything that will help me feel less tired.

You know?

I think we're taught not to complain because it's a blessing. And it is. Of course. Of course. But all these tiny little things that add up over time. All of them fill you up. To the brim. And it's hard to carry that around with you all the time you know?

Because really I've spent my whole life hating my body. Honestly. And then actually when I was pregnant I didn't mind it. It was doing something purposeful. And the roundness stretched out the bumps you know? It looked beautiful actually. But now I've done that twice I've got this utter wreck of a thing that keeps malfunctioning and no matter how many times I tell myself I'm proud of it and what it did and what it gave me I just.

Oh of course there were probably loads of things I could do but there were also many other things that I had to do instead. And really why would I have ever prioritised my body and its needs when I've hated it for so long? Of course I fucking didn't.

My littlest sometimes pokes my naked tummy when I get out of the shower and says something about how big and wobbly it is. And I say, I say 'Well yes darling but that big wobbly thing grew two babies. I grew you and your brother and isn't it wonderful? What a clever tummy.'

I want to believe what I say to my children about my body. But years and years of conditioning about it and how disgusting it is doesn't just disappear. And this lovely woman who only minutes ago had her fingers up me is looking at me with such gentle understanding. And I know I'm not the first woman to break down in her surgery. And I know I could patch myself up in some way if I really wanted to. And if it was my daughter I would want her to.

The session ended and I went home and made tea and did bathtime and bedtime and kissed my children goodnight and ran a bath for myself and forgot to get in it and instead just sat in front of the telly and watched something really shit and then went to bed too late and got up at about six and did breakfast and the school run and then sat down at my desk to work and stared at the sheet of paper she gave me with all the exercises on and didn't do them and then it was the end of the day and I had to make tea again.

I really truly want to believe what I say to my children about my body. But.

I think I'm just really, really tired.

BABY YOGA

Suhayla El-Bushra

Performed by Tsion Habte
Directed by Tim Hoare

Director of Photography Crusoe Weston
Editor Ali White and Linda Gurski
Sound Technician Tom Moore
Focus Puller Moses Jeremiah
Colour Tim Martin

Cricklewood, 2005.

SHIREEN

She's changed. Like, I knew she would, obviously. I knew she'd be fat and that her tits would be MASSIVE but I wasn't expecting.

I went to call for her yesterday. I skinned up beforehand cos I had a bit of that teenth left and it was sunny so why the fuck not? I stopped off at Food Mart for one of those big bags of fake Wotsits and a Guava Rubicon. She said she'd probably just get a salad later. I was like 'What the fuck Jasmine? Salad?' and she was all 'Yeah it goes into your breast milk you need the nutrients.'

I was heading towards Gladstone but she wanted to go Queen's Park, 'for the café'? I said okay, even though Queen's Park is a nightmare to get high in, cos it's so open, plus it's always like properly rammed.

We get down there and it's full of women and babies. Not like Jasmine, with hers in a sling. They've all got these special prams. Bugaboo or whatever. And they've parked them in formation, like fucking army tanks or something. And the women are dressed identically, in exercise clothes, but not like the old leggings you find scrunched up at the back of your drawer, I'm talking seriously high-grade Paltrow shit.

And I'm like 'Jesus what is this a cult or something?' And she's like 'It's just some mother-and-baby yoga thing.' And I'm like 'Mother-and-baby yoga? Is this who you are now?' And she starts laughing. She's all 'Don't be dumb it's like twenty pound a session.' So we sneak up and join in on the sly and we're trying not to piss ourselves because it's fucking hilarious, but then one of the women spots us and comes over. Like, it's not even her class. And she goes 'Some of us have actually paid to do this?' and I'm like, 'Yeah, twenty quid they saw you coming.' She notices the spliff tucked behind my ear and says 'I hope you're not planning on smoking that near the baby,' so I'm like 'Who the fuck are you, Social Services?' And Jasmine's all 'Come on Shireen let's go,' but I really don't like the way this woman is looking at me.

She's got this full-on bitch face. Like she's blonde, with these clear blue eyes and she's got that make-up on where it's not obvious you're wearing make-up but you look good, and that's all anyone needs to know. And she's fit, like she might have just had a baby but her body is tight. Not like Jasmine's. And Jasmine's only sixteen this woman's gotta be what, forty? She looks good but she's properly old.

So I'm standing there and she's looking at me like she's going to call the police or something, just because I'm sitting in the park with a fucking joint in my hair. And everything about her is making me want to smash her face in, when the baby starts to cry. And Jasmine's trying to shush it but it's not working so she starts trying to feed it, only it's like really awkward cos the baby's thrashing around so much she can't get her boob in its mouth. And the woman's just staring at her and in the end she goes 'Here' and she grabs the baby's head and she just kind of tilts it and whacks it onto Jasmine's tit and the thing shuts up. And Jasmine's finally still and it's only then that I notice she's crying. And the woman just looks at her and goes 'Prozac. But not while you're breastfeeding.' And then she walks off.

I figure now is probably a good time to spark up the doobie, right? Only Jasmine's all 'What is wrong with you?' She moves out the way like I'm blowing smoke on the baby even though I'm nowhere fucking near it. I can see the woman looking at me while she talks to her friend giving me fucking evils. And I'm like 'What is her problem?' and Jasmine's all 'Fuck's sake Shireen. I'm going to get something to eat.'

I watch her walk off as I smoke. I can hear music playing on someone's car radio. It's that fucking James Blunt song which I officially hate but actually in the sun, in my haze, I'm almost enjoying it in a weird way. And then it ends and it's the news and I hear how there's been like three bombings on the Tube, and I'm like fuck, man. This is serious. And I look over at the café and I see Jasmine with the baby and some massive plate of leaves in front of her and she looks so far away from me. And I'm wondering if they've got the radio on in the café and if so has she heard and would she even care or is that fucking baby all that matters right now? Cos I honestly can't imagine her giving two fucks.

I look up and see the yoga women heading over to the café. That bitch shoots me a look. I hear her say she needs to put more money on the car, so I watch as she goes up to some shiny big beast of a thing. She walks up to the café and I see her stop at Jasmine's table and say something, and the two of them smile. And I think I haven't seen Jasmine smile for ages, not properly.

I'm looking at her and thinking fuck's sake are you actually gonna come back out and sit with me or are you just gonna stop in there with those women and their lattes and salad and shit while the world burns around your fucking ears? She is you know. She only fucking is.

I get up and I leave the park. And I walk over to that bitch's fancy SUV. And I take out my lipstick. And I write the word CUNT in massive letters across her windscreen. I don't know why it makes me feel better about everything. It just does.

UNTOLD

Jodi Gray

Performed by Zainab Hasan
Directed by Jennifer Tang

Director of Photography   Sam Traviss
Editor   Sam Traviss and Ali White
Sound Designer   George Lloyd-Burman
Sound Technician   Tom Anderson
Camera Assistant   Linda Gurski

Note on Text

Words in [square brackets] are intention, and not to be spoken.

So, hey –

So hey it's been a year. Give or take. Just over. Just under a year.

You see me playing it cool like I don't know the exact date.

Cuz actually I know them all. Every date. Every stage of our – 'togetherness'. So, then, the truth is that it's been just over a year since *you*. And just under a year since we went our separate ways.

I was a bit surprised by you, I think it's fair to say! Surprised or. Unprepared, certainly. My defences were – mm – lower, than I would have liked.

Unprotected, I was.

You were a dizzy moment of feeling of something, some possibility of something, an idea of myself that I had maybe put aside or not believed in and – yes, then, unbelievably, *you*. Undeniably here. And believe you me, I tried to deny [it]. Desperately. But. In the end, what good did that do either of us?

…

I'm wondering, about context – because people like context, don't they? Like, what if this is confusing because they don't know me and they don't know what to make of me. And I don't want to be confusing because I, now I know how it feels to be unconfused. So – context:

…

I'll tell you about me before you. I'm – let's be honest – older than I imagined that I would be. Ever. Not like I thought I would be dead by now (was never particularly death-defying), but as in, when I imagined being a grown-up? Wasn't this. I was, like, twenty-five, tops. Without these guys – (*Re: crow's feet and/or other lines on her face.*) without these – (*Re: vaguely wobbly upper arms; maybe cellulite.*) It never struck me as possible that I would be this age. Or at least – this age and the particular Me that I am:

This me that is – yes, well, *alone*. Technically, 'alone', but actually – 'solo', so: unaccompanied. Mm – accurate!

And this is because I (like so many *little girls*) have been peddled just the one option and offered only the one *desire*. No one ever told me that This Me, this Solo Me, was, was something I might, could, want. Might could be okay. Always seemed so fucking *transgressive*. To wonder – what else could I be?

And everybody telling me, like they love to tell women like me, like they *need to tell* us – It will happen for you! Don't worry! And I would think, I'm not worried! Either way! But I would never say that. (People do not want to hear that you are not worried about being an unaccompanied woman. All the foot-looseness and fancy-freeness is *threatening*. I am a threat, apparently! So I keep my self-sufficiency *to* myself, dangerous as it is.) I say Thank you! and Fingers crossed! And watch another bouquet sail happily ever after over my head – There she goes!

I don't want to gross you out but I actually I really like sex. It's one of the few things that make me remember I have a body. Sex is, even when it's not very good, it's still so wonderfully – tangible. I really like sex with people I don't know very well. Oh hey look: I also like sex with people I do know, a bit, or quite well, but it's always messier. And sex is messy enough. If you're doing it right, haha! Um, I find intimacy confusing, is what I think I mean. And overwhelming. And.

Overrated.

It makes me self-conscious, I think is what it is. And when I'm self-conscious, I can't be in my body, and if I'm not in my body then sex is pointless. Like, in my experience, you have sex with someone more than about three times and all of a sudden there's something or some expectation of something, even if no one is

expecting anything there is the *expectation of* the expectation of
something. And I do not like people expecting things of me,
I find it, frankly, unnerving.

'What do you want?' You know?! 'CAN'T YOU LEAVE ME
ALONE?

For a *second*?'

(*Small laugh.*)

So I'm saying: me, personally, it's not, it doesn't work for me,
I can't be free *and* intimate. Or intimate and free, whichever
way – But hey lots of women can! There's millions of them out
there what can! So I think it's okay if I can't. I have my weird
little niche and I'm very happy here.

...

*I wonder am I coming off like a bitch? And after that I wonder,
is it better if I do? Sort of: Maybe if I present this particular
woman as missing some vital 'woman-ness' – so: defective – if
I keep telling them how awful I am, will they understand me?
Judge me.*

...

Some people actually like to be consumed by someone else. To
be taken over. I think that sounds like actual *insanity*, not gonna
lie, it sounds disgusting.

What I think I'm trying to tell you is that I can't think of
anything more all-consuming, more intimate than you. And if
it's intimate then I would be hurt maybe, so. I mean, sure,
Hello, classic commitmentphobe! I'm not claiming, you know,
any *originality* here, with this. It's not interesting. I'm not an
interesting person. You would have found me very boring, in
the end. Boring and embarrassing and disappointing.

But then who isn't embarrassed and disappointed by their
parents?! – Ah, 'lol'.

I did two tests in the morning, one using my first morning wee
because that's got more, I dunno, more concentrated

information in it, something like that. And then I also went to my doctor and got my doctor to do one, because that's what people do in films and on TV, but actually, the doctor said the home kits are so accurate now it's not even necessary. Really I wanted her to tell me I was dreaming.

But she didn't tell me that. She just asked, quite simply: 'And is this – *good news*?' And here's me digging my nails into my palms so I wake up and I won't have to say the word –

'No.'

Spent my whole life, before you, not particularly wanting anything, okay. Or needing, you know. Or making decisions. Or being definite. When I was younger I was surprised when people recognised me, because I saw myself – when I looked in the mirror, which I didn't very much, it didn't seem relevant – I saw myself as so non-descript as to be, like, *beneath notice*. My face seemed to me blurred, and in photos I am just a smudge of someone turning fast away from the camera.

We didn't get to know each other very well so this is me filling in the blanks of myself for you, so you can feel better about not wanting me.

And look you can't deny it, I could tell you didn't want me because I was sick, all the time – morning, afternoon, nightly, despite what they tell you. It's not a good sign can't be a *good* sign. Can it. That you made me so sick. It's a sign that you weren't overly happy about the situation either. Both of us kinda rebelling, physically, and saying: Imagine being stuck and stuck with me. Can you imagine anything worse?

So when the doctor asked: 'What do you want to do?'

I spent a lot of time thinking about the point of myself. Because – So, other women seem to have this *point* to them, an absolute certainty, this laser-focus, you know. So *sure* –

But with you it was like my *not wanting* of you was the most sure I'd ever been about anything, ever. I'm not being flippant, cuz it was actually amazing, to me – So when people said to me Are you sure? I could truthfully say I've never been So Sure about anything in my life! And what's incredible is, now that I know I have it in me to be So Sure, I wonder what I might be So Sure about next?!

Yeah, so. So I would like to thank you for that. For certainty. I hope that's not too hurtful. Don't wanna be an actual dick about it but I'm telling you and telling you all this so that you know that my decision to end it was a good decision and the one, the only one that made any kind of *sense*. You're not mine and you never were.

…

And I wonder: Am I allowed to mourn? I think I probably am. But I don't want to, is that – ?

I will properly look like a bitch. For sure.

Well – fuck it.

…

I want you to know that you have made me definite. Yeah. And so I'm grateful. You're the best thing that ever didn't happen to me!

I'm *in here*, now. (*She means in her body.*)

I just really wanted to tell you that.

(*End.*)

VENUS OF WHITECHAPEL

Naomi Sheldon

Performed by Naomi Sheldon
Directed by Annabel Arden

Director of Photography   Crusoe Weston
Editor   Crusoe Weston and Ali White
Sound Designer   Abraham Moughrabi
Creative Consultant   Jack Jeffreys
Colour   Tim Martin

There are magpies outside my bedroom window every day now and they are getting very loud.

One for sorrow, two for joy.

I get these headaches.

It happened very easily. Too easily really, if I'm allowed, if it's not impolite, not ungrateful to say. I think it took about five, about five or... it was bloody quick.

There was a great deal of focus on the actual, the moment of the conception. He didn't know but it absolutely had to be perfect. I got this idea in my head that to make a child, a really good one, the sex should be pretty much the best most moving sex in which two people really, to borrow from the Spice Girls, become one. Orgasm ideally and if so nothing too over the top, very polite, you know.

But I had this sense, this *feeling* that it wouldn't be easy. People struggle for years, trying and trying, and succeeding and losing and trying again, very brave. Friends of mine, the podcasts, *Woman's Hour*, they told me what to expect. Longing, you know? The longing seems particularly –

...

So I'd really signed up to that. Maybe a year, maybe two, then we'd decide that after all this wasn't for us. We'd travel to Japan. Take risks. Eat a poisonous delicious fish. Have that big night out on MDMA. Sample a sex party. Or four.

But after five, yeah about five... highly pressured sex situations, I fainted on Oxford Street and... *voilà*. Just like that. *Just like that*.

So quick I was convinced I'd lose them. It seemed too lucky... I hadn't worried enough to warrant this luck. Rebecca deserved it, Elinor, Elizabeth, Lewis, Lauren, Sian, Polly, Lucy, Sarah

One and Sarah Two, good good people. So why this good fortune (and not just one, it's two, it's twins) this abundance of babies showering down on me?

It's because I have a different fate. Something worse around the corner, a terrible tragedy. No I see, I see. That makes a lot of sense.

So I set myself milestones where I can take a quick breath before diving again into

Twelve weeks

the fear

Sixteen weeks

do you want to know the sexes?

Eighteen weeks

first twitches, then a swooshing, are they? Yes they're moving

Twenty weeks

but the stakes keep getting higher and instead of the fear diminishing

Twenty-five weeks

I'm convinced I'm in for a tragedy

Thirty weeks

of epic proportions

These islands of safety are not as helpful as I'd thought. It occurs to me I'll rely on them for the rest of my life. Plunging out of hope and back into fear.

The magpies keep me up at dawn. We wake simultaneously. Them cackling. My head stuck out of the window, gasping for air.

I know there isn't a value system in place I know you don't *earn* (or not earn) a baby, but at the same time I'm not convinced I deserve one. Two. I think of them as I might a brilliant idea. They enter my mind and then if I don't act quickly enough, can't execute the... the concept properly, they will visit someone else. Someone brighter, with more ability, more capability, someone who has longed.

The midwives see me coming a mile off. I'm all apologetic smiles but there's a wild glint in my eye. This one's trouble.

'I'm sorry about this, I'm so sorry but I do have a couple, just a few silly questions...' unrolling my list of very specific researched queries dragged from academic articles from a particularly dusty corner of the internet on lung development.

Sympathetic eyes but I can't tell what their mouths are doing.

'It's a textbook pregnancy. Absolutely nothing to be worried about. No indications that anything might go wrong. You should relax.'

Relax. Relax. Relax. I sense the mouth alter, tightening perhaps

'And if you don't relax your stress hormones could affect the babies.'

Everyone is telling me

'You look very well'

Really?

'You're glowing'

I'm hot, my feet have expanded

'Nice neat bump'

into butcher's slabs

'Clever girl'

What is a messy bump, exactly?

But there's barely time to think about this because before I know it, I've ballooned. I'm obscenely proportioned. I am all tits and belly. I shouldn't work. When I turn, I keep on turning, there's no end to me, a glorious planet of flesh and life.

I search out mirrors, a reflection of any kind is most welcome at this time. Shadows are particularly mesmerising.

I am all vanity.

Strong, pony-like muscles in my legs prop up this new appendage. Stretch marks, the sumptuous fat on my arms on my thighs, obscene nipples. My body my own and yet not my own. I'm always calling him to come and look. Have you seen this?

I am so full of babies.

Only inches from my fingertips. Think of that! A bit of skin, some muscle, fat and then there they are. Two living human beings. There's a reason I can't fully understand it: self-preservation, I'd lose my mind. I'm not *meant* to comprehend this. My children exist, I just can't see them. Absolutely not. It's bananas.

At the physio, this pain again, ribs falling apart, I'm asked

'And how's Mum doing?'

It takes a moment but I realise Mum is me.

When did I become a mother? At what point precisely? Was it when their cells first divided? Or now, now I feel the kicking, butterfly feet stabbing me hard in the, yes that's my, that's my cervix. Confirmation that someone somewhere is telling me they exist.

Oh I'm fine, I say, my belly button will never be the same again! I don't tell her that I've just realised that I'm not worried about losing them any more. They are now more real than me.

I listen to the meditations every day. A religion. Empowered birth something something anxiety calm the fuck down and breathe. It tells me about automatic processes. How my heart beats, my blood circulates, my lungs pull in air. All without me ever having to know exactly how it happens. You just don't have to think about it. Trust your body. It tells me.

I have my dawn date with the magpies. Head out of the window. They cackle. Hips throbbing. I expand and expand. My pelvis is now two tectonic plates drifting apart. The ache in my ribs has changed. Just under the shoulder blades, I feel the muscles begin to rip. My eyes are trained on the birds. One for sorrow, two for joy, three for a girl, four for a boy.

Everything fills me with dread.

I should know how to care for them, it shouldn't be news that I don't wash them in the first two weeks of life (don't they start to smell that way?). I should know what the golden oil is that has started staining my satin dressing gown I can't get the marks out I can't get the marks out.

Huge belly resists being covered by stained gown, looks ridiculous, I am all belly, all breasts, all leakage. I ooze into every environment. Ooze my way as fat feet slap pavements, shifting monumentally from hip to hip after all *I am pregnant* (I let my body boom), and I will take up space. I ooze with impunity.

I post a picture of myself on Instagram. Big belly, legs crossing at the juncture of pubic hair, the merest hint of the underside of heavy breasts. Arty. I make a joke about constipation but I'm leaning into Demi Moore and everyone knows it.

Goddess

Mama Warrior

Lioness

Thirst Trap

You are so powerful

I am so vulnerable. My skin has peeled off. I am a disembodied assembly of distended stomach and swollen breasts, the nipples gargantuan, the thighs ropes of bark. I have become a fertility symbol. Venus of Willendorf. All bulbous body and receding head.

I'm searching for a picture of my mum, my mum pregnant, but there aren't any and I wonder why she hasn't documented this period. Perhaps it wasn't done in 1985, perhaps it was uncouth, perhaps she didn't need to, perhaps she understood that she was pregnant and she didn't need the evidence thank you very much, that'll come when she has the child in her arms. Very practical see. Very self-assured.

My babies are so real they make my belly ripple when they do somersaults inside me. Womb astronauts. I stare at my little black-and-white scans sitting on my desk. Both of them grinning. They are not going anywhere. They are solid.

The meditation tonight asks me to notice if I'm holding on. It asks me to let go. It asks me to sink deeper and deeper into nothingness. Sinking down until I can't feel my body. Can't hear thoughts. Breathing deeply. Sinking further. There's some initial resistance from my heart. It pumps hard. Fight or flight. Then a softening.

Dawn. My friends eye me cautiously. Balaclavas pulled over white breasts.

This time when I gasp for air there is a crack. The muscle that connected rib to rib has parted. Lightning pain but I've been preparing for this for months. My threshold has built up. I heave my heavy hips onto the window ledge, look back at my sleeping partner and what remains of me curled up in a complex arrangement of pillows. I want to hesitate, reconsider, but the body is ahead of me. Trust it, trust it. My thick thighs shake, my wide feet steady. I take me and my babies into the sky and with terrific strength beat my thick ancient wings. Feathers fluttering in the morning air.

THE QUEEN'S HEAD

Katherine Kotz

Performed by Katherine Kotz
Directed by Elin Schofield

Director of Photography　Crusoe Weston
Editor　Ali White
Thanks to Sal Bunker

A WOMAN *is in a therapy session.*

Thank you for seeing me. I had a sort of… episode at work.

(*Flashback to the woman doing a presentation to colleagues via Zoom:*)

Hello, Birmingham team! It's been so long hasn't it. Great to see you all. Now I haven't actually presented on Zoom before so you'll have to bear with me. Let's take you all off mute for a start, I don't want this to be a lecture…

You're a noisy bunch, aren't you! I can hear some quite loud chewing actually… perhaps I will just mute you after all.

Where've you gone? Can you still hear me? Oh I've muted you haven't I.

There we are, we're back.

Right! Where were we. Ah. Yes. Okay I can see some raised eyebrows so let's address the elephant in the room. Which is me, isn't it. I'm the elephant.

Yes. I'm pregnant. It's not a big deal. Why are you all looking at me like that?

(*Back in the therapy session:*)

They were looking at me like I'd just told them I had three months to live… like they wanted to *hug* me or something.

(*In the Zoom presentation:*)

Guys, this isn't *who I am* now, okay? This is just something that happens to people. I'm not going to be lolloping into the office in dungarees, chattering about sleep cycles with an arse like a sad curtain.

Sorry Karen.

(*Back in the therapy session:*)

I mean Mark should be carrying this baby, not me. He hates his job. Any excuse to sit down, that's Mark. Not a great quality in a paramedic. God, he'd love being pregnant. Time off work, showing the bump to his mates down the pub, eating for four in case it's triplets.

(*In the Zoom presentation:*)

It's so unfair! I love my job. I need to be here. And now they've got Luci with an 'i' to cover my maternity leave. Who can't even spell her own name. They've got their eye on me for redundancy I know they have. Yes I can see you smirking, Alan.

Some women never go back to work after having kids. You know that, don't you? No one will employ them. They just... wander the streets, do a bit in the garden, volunteer in a charity shop, and then die.

(*Back in the therapy session:*)

In the end it got quite ugly. I think it was the hormones.

(*In the Zoom presentation:*)

Haven't women done enough? Isn't it time we had a little sodding siesta from all the baby-making, and home-keeping, and trying not to offend anyone. I mean what is science playing at. They can clone people, but they can't give men some ovaries and the ability to notice when the bathroom needs a clean?

(*Back in the therapy session:*)

They were really enjoying it by this point. Alan had microwaved some popcorn.

(*In the Zoom presentation:*)

In the end... it all comes down to THIS doesn't it, ladies and gentlemen. (*She scrawls a massive cock and balls on the flip chart.*) IF YOU DON'T HAVE ONE OF THESE, YOU'RE F**KED.

(*Back in the therapy session:*)

I think I'm a bit conflicted about the pregnancy.

I wasn't convinced it was a good idea at first. Sharing your body for nine months with a total stranger? What if they turn out to be an arsehole? Michael Gove was a baby.

I spent the first two days of the pregnancy googling 'women who regret having children'. Mark found me curled up on the bath mat naked, cheeks stained with mascara, watching highlights from the *Antiques Roadshow*. He was very sweet. Just prised the phone from my grip and lay on top of me like a support animal. Said we'd work out what to do.

Sometimes I feel this intense rush of love towards him, and all I can think about is him dying violently in an accident. Is that normal?

(*No response.*)

We flipped a coin.

Not as a contractual obligation, just to give us that gut reaction, you know. Whichever side it landed on, we'd know how we felt.

The Queen's head told us to have the baby. God, the relief! I've kept the coin for her eighteenth. *This coin saved your life.* Would it be weird to hear that?

The thing is, I've never been remotely interested in babies. That *instinct* that's supposed to reside in women, you know, that makes them go all doe-eyed when they look at a tiny cardigan. It's never been there in me. And I can't help but think, how many people have kids because they think they should?

I suppose I just want to know if it's normal? To have doubts? My friends all said 'You need to be sure, it's a massive decision'. But how can you be sure when you don't know what it's going to be like?

I've always thought babies were just noisy and leaky and an infringement on your basic human rights. But it's weird... now this one's here, moving around inside me, with her own brain and eyelids and fingernails... fucking fingernails! I feel... protective. And I think: who is this person? What will she be like? To create a human. I mean, that's amazing... isn't it?

A LETTER TO MY BABY

Anya Reiss

Performed by Tom Rhys Harries
Directed by Sam Phillips and Anya Reiss

Director of Photography   Crusoe Weston
Editor   Ali White

First published by Oberon Books, London, in 2019
in *My White Best Friend* (*and Other Letters Left Unsaid*)
edited by Rachel De-lahay

There is a bag on stage. Please wear what is inside. (It's a pair of red trousers.)

Pick up envelope, read what's on the back of it.

A note from the writer:

The writer would like to acknowledge that though she does indeed have a baby and this is a letter to a baby, it should not necessarily be construed as being written to THE baby, rather A baby.

Or as the back of a DVD case the writer has just found says 'any resemblance to actual persons, living or dead, or actual events is purely coincidental'.

PS Please don't take my baby.

He's my friend.

(Open the envelope. Take out your letter. And read. Out loud.)

Dear Baby Boy,

You are one years old. This is not a letter of the unsaid. This is said. I say this to you. You just don't say anything back. You can be an asshole like that.

But as soon as you can answer I will stop saying this.

Because you can't know.

You can't know that I think I might not be the best. You can't know that sometimes you make me mad. And sometimes you annoy me. And sometimes I wish you weren't here.

You put your hands down the toilet. You chew on wires. You throw things out the bin. You turn the TV off while I'm watching. You throw food on the floor.

The food on the floor really pisses me off.

You cry when I don't let you smash my laptop on the ground. You broke my phone. You pull my hair. You gouge my eyes. You lost the TV remote for three days. I could only get onto Hayu on Amazon. I watched the whole of the *Real Housewives of Beverly Hills* again.

You made me do that.

I'm stupider now than I was before. And you are to blame.

I didn't want to be one of those white, middle-class mums you see smiling as they eat a garden salad and their kid screams and spits on them.

I wanted to be strict.

I wanted to be badass.

I wanted to be Lisa Vanderpump.

Or maybe Erika Giradi.

They're from the *Real Housewives*. Look what you've done to me.

I wanted a son with maximum respect.

I wanted to be a Ghanaian mum.

I wanted to be Daniel's mum. Daniel's Ghanaian mum. You did not fuck with that woman. I'd shout at my mum and Daniel'd be so confused. I want that.

But when I shout, you get cross.

When I stop you, you are confused.

If I cry, you think I'm laughing and you laugh. I wish that made me laugh. I bet good mums laugh. But I don't. I just cry more.

There is so much talk of being the perfect mum. Of how Instagram and Mumsnet has made us doubt ourselves and compete. How 'mums are superheroes'. But 'mums are only human'.

Fuck that, I thought.

Who are these sad women, comparing their parenting skills?
I'm never going to do that. I actually have a life.

I'm just going to be…

quietly

fucking

amazing.

I'm not an honest person. I never have been. I wanted to be an
actor as a child. Pretend to be someone else. Those bitches are
amateurs. I went one further. I became a writer. I'm not just a
liar. I cram my lies into other people's mouths. I marshal my
differing opinions and confused thoughts and throw it out there
so I don't have to confront a thing.

But then there is fucking Rachel.

With *My White Best Friend*.

Being honest. Being truthful. Here I am trying to give that a go.

Like I say baby boy, and you will learn this, honesty is not my
strongest suit.

I'm shocked I'm not a better mum. I'm shocked I'm not a better
person really. I always thought I was and I am just starting to
learn that I'm not.

And that sucks.

But hey, baby, know why I had you. I lay in bed with the bright
sunlight coming through my blinds on a hangover and thought
'Enough of this now, y'know what a baby would stop me doing
this shit.'

But here I am.

And here you are.

And I'm still ██████████████████████

I'm going to █████████████████████████████
██████████

Number one. I dropped you when I was drunk.

Number two. You pulled my hair so I screamed in your face. An inch from your face. You cried.

Hang on, sorry. I just looked up bad-mum confessions on the internet to get some inspiration. Someone 'admitted' they let the baby sleep in the car seat and another 'let their baby have pretzels for dinner'. Now I'm embarrassed.

Looking at you over there as I type,

with your cold breakfast pizza.

Gonna stop that confessional tract right there. Better get back to lying.

Is everyone going to hate white people by the end of this? We were pretty bad by the end of Rachel's monologue. And now. Good God. Look at the state of the white person in this one. If my bad parenting incites a race war I will have peaked.

Now baby boy do not get me wrong. I love you very much. I have no regrets in having you. My regrets are all turned inwards. You are my mirror and I don't like what I see.

I've also given you a terrible haircut.

So I literally do not like what I see either.

I saw a therapist,

in this fictional universe where any resemblance to actual persons, living or dead, is purely coincidental,

and I told the therapist I would be happy whoever you turned out to be.

We were talking about my mum see and the terrible traumas inflicted upon me when she wouldn't let me wear trainers that flashed when you stamped.

And my God I wanted some trainers that flashed when you stamped.

And I told the therapist my mum had a lot of rules like that, she didn't want me to pretend to be someone I wasn't. Which the therapist countered with, 'But you were a child, how did you know who you *was* and *wasn't?*'

Were.

I silently corrected in my head.

'That was about her,' my fictional not-at-all-real therapist said, 'that was about who she wanted her kid to be.'

Oh the revelation that happened to me, baby boy! The Damascus road awakening of the terrible parenting that had been inflicted upon me, suddenly all my bad behaviour is validated! And of course I drop you when I'm drunk because I'm not a bad person just a very very traumatised trainer-less child.

How can a parent have so little sense of self that their child becomes their accessory? How weak and fragile an ego that extends the expectations they have for themselves onto their poor innocent child?

You know what I told that not-at-all-real therapist, baby boy? I told that therapist that you could be anything.

You can be a meth-addicted parking warden squatting on a houseboat with your gay lover Raoul. I don't care, baby boy! You be you! I am a cheerleader to your life. I love you no matter fucking what.

Because that's the deal of a parent isn't it?

Unconditional love.

And I get that and I'm signed up for that.

'What if ' –

my-totally-fictional-therapist-who-in-no-way-seems-to-penetrate-my-well-constructed-woke-liberal-front

'What if ' –

she asked

or he

either

they're not real

'What if he was… a county vet in red trousers?'

And suddenly, baby boy. Suddenly.

There I am.

I can hear the crunch of gravel under the tyres in the drizzling rain as we meander up the driveway to the detached pebbledashed three-bedroom house in Surrey.

I can hear the two labradoodles,

they're hypoallergenic don't you know

barking already.

Francis and Zelda.

Named after the Scott Fitzgeralds even though I know you've only read *The Great Gatsby* briefly at school, are yappy and never have their nails – claws?

– what the fuck do you even call them on a dog –

cut and they jump up, leaving muddy pawprints across me.

You sigh and laugh as you run out after them, you look a little out of breath, sorry, you explain you were trying to force Zelda to eat her ham roll. It contains her medicine. The dog's diabetic.

Because of course it fucking is.

I look you over baby boy and say it's good to see you, yes you laugh and pat your stomach. Little too much maybe. I had noticed. I glance down at the slightly see-through white shirt straining at the top of *those* trousers that don't have a zip but only buttons. I don't know why they're made like that. And you call for your wife, call her away from 'the coal face'

which is what you call cooking.

On an Aga.

And I greet Jenny, as best I can.

'Mothers and their sons,' you say at dinner parties, about me and my daughter-in-law. 'No woman's ever good enough for their son.' And everyone nods and agrees because of course, that is why I don't like Jenny.

Of course,

that's the reason.

And out Jenny comes in her comfortable home Crocs and toenails that have not been cut and if they were would fly across the room like missiles because they're best described as chunky.

'Come on in folks!' she cries. 'I'm making gammon.'

.

.

.

.

Your father's here.

We make pleasant conversation.

I make a witty, if snide, remark about the kids who are either on their iPads or drawing on the actual table and he cuts me down about my constant need to judge others.

A quality I've always been rather fond of, but apparently is ugly… especially in old age. He says.

But we're all playing nice because it's our son's birthday and our grandkids have made him some lopsided mug and even the tennis coach sent a card.

The conversation turns to politics. I don't say anything. I try to talk to the children instead. I try to not hear what's being said. But I hear it all the same.

Your baby has cradle cap. Jenny says it doesn't need treatment, babies just grow out of it. I can see it from across the table. All the children have snot bubbling out their noses. You don't do anything. They're blonde and have gingham trousers on. You say how cute they are. Your babies make you very happy.

And you, *my* baby boy, sit proudly at the head of your table. You carve the incredibly fatty meat and spoon home-grown parsnips onto plates that were a real find in that flea market in Paris that you and Jenny went to ten years ago on your last 'kid-free' holiday, and – and – and –

And as you can see, baby boy.

I am.

.

Fine.

.

With this.

I'd be fine.

If you were like that.

No…

no…

no judgement.

At all.

.

I seem to have finally separated my ego from myself, but now it's all over there, all sitting with you, and Lord knows I do not trust you with it.

My baby boy, out there, my mirror, that I can no longer control and I must not judge. Just out there reflecting me. This constant mirror satellite of myself, holding all my identity, but with none of my say-so. Just wandering round the world.

Being you.

Because parents should love their kids, and I know I'd love my kid no matter…

No matter…

What.

I'd love my kid no matter what.

I just really hope you're a meth-head gay boy.

Not…

The actor looks down to the trousers he was given. Back to the letter.

And there's a real chance

With your dad

There's a real chance that you might be…

But you love your kid no matter what.

So…

Throw your food on the floor. Smash at the TV with wet hands. Chew up that pizza crust and try and feed it back to me.

My beautiful little man.

Because.

It seems.

It could.

It might.

Only get worse from here.

NUMBER 1

E.V. Crowe

Performed by Landry Adelard
Directed by Tim Hoare

Director of Photography   Crusoe Weston
Editor   Ali White
Sound Technician   Tom Anderson
Camera Assistant   Rory Ronnie
Thanks to Ollie Dahmen

1.

Come in sit down.

He's fucking my mum.

Oh my gosh.

Come in sit down.

Who do you want?

Put your pen down. Listen.

Who do you think you want?

(Pause.)

We think about it.

I say the one with the red case.

Good idea, nice ide-a.

He says don't piss about in my class.

Are you pissing about?

I'm not – FUCKOFF.

2.

Bell and they come out.

Who d'you come up with?

I'm keen.

Alistair Darling?

Wha?

Or manager at a bank.

Wha?

Or trader at Canary Wharf.

Cool.

David Beckham.

–

Who we getting then?

Who then?

(*'Number 1' by Tinchy Stryder plays.*)

Star-in-the-Hood-Stryder? Oh, come on. Come on.

I was into that track for like a week, that's old now.

And why do they think we want Tinchy to come down here give us his pearls of?

I'm taller than Tinchy.

Fuck Tinchy man.

If he's so business, why's he got time to come to our school. I bet he's 'sexting' Miss Streatham.

Not that I don't not want to meet him.

I am quite excited about meeting Tinchy Stryder.

Oh my gosh.

Tinchy was my suggestion. I would have suggested that.

Come on. (*Hums the track.*) That was a good song. Come on.

3.

Come in sit down.

He's fucking my mum. She's saying '*This is my boyfriend.*'

Come in sit down.

Shut the door.

I've had a report.

None of the girls can come in tomorrow until we've unblocked them.

They're all blocked up.

It's health and safety. That they can't come in. Thanks to you.

The Room 7 girls won't get to meet Tinchy Stryder. Or to learn about Personal Finance on our Personal Finance Day with Tinchy Stryder. And their books are stuck down the girls' toilets.

You definitely won't get to meet Mr Stryder. Tinchy says 'more important than making money is looking after your money'. Do you know about interest rates, Tinchy rates?

I can google it, can't I?

You're excluded for tomorrow.

Miss Streatham wants to know why you did it.

Oh my gosh.

Look at Miss Streatham.

Because when you give a girl a job she will get pregnant. Eventually. It's true. They do. They do. And then she'll fuck it up. So I thought, flush their books.

Classroom 7 girls could just be on PlayStation. Or something. All day.

Don't they deserve learning too? That's Miss Streatham asking.

– What's the point? Really.

Miss S looks sad face.

4.

My mum.

She can come in and talk.

About being a successful woman.

Does she have a job?

She had a job yeah. Before.

Okay.

Why your mum?

She's a successful woman. My mum.

In what way is she a successful woman?

I don't understand. She doesn't have a number-one record called 'Number 1'. She's not Tinchy Stryder. I'm not saying my mum is Tinchy Stryder.

Oh my gosh.

She's just like, I don't know, you said I had to do something to say sorry. To the Classroom 7 girls.

She can talk about being successful.

Okay.

Okay. Cool.

5.

Other mums come in also.

They call it a 'be nice to women day'. Or someshit.

A women's day. Like for girls. Cool, cool.

Yeh-yeh-yeah.

They talk about being on the till, or being a PA for a big bank, or being a nurse. What that is like.

Where's your mum?

(*Pause.*)

I don't know.

Where's your successful mum?

I actually don't know.

I do know.

I don't know actually.

Don't be a girl about this. The school office can give her a call to remind her.

I won't try calling. No need.

She can't reach the phone.

I know it.

You can't get to the phone from the radiator. No way.

Silence.

She is bike-locked to the radiator until the afternoon.

This is my boyfriend. He's moving in.

I'm Lee. I'm moving in.

Why is she bike-locked to the radiator?

(*Pause.*)

Oh my gosh, I don't know. It makes it easier?

Ask *him*. Lee.

Tell him... tell him...

(*Pause.*)

...If he can go do the lock quick she might make it in, in time to do her talk after the other mums.

She can say something quick.

I even don't know what it is she was going to talk about.

I just wanted her to say something.

About being

A successful person.

I wanted my mum to say something about that I think she is a successful person.

Doesn't matter. She couldn't make it this one time.

I just wanted my mum to say something.

I wanted my mum to say something about that I think she is a successful person.

Sort of. My.

Number One.

(*Sings the chorus of 'Number 1' by Tinchy Stryder*.)

(*Pause*.)

Oh my gosh.

(*End*.)

GUNK

Irenosen Okojie

Performed by Sarah Niles
Directed by Akinola Davies Jr.

Sound Designer   Abraham Moughrabi
Thanks to Lucian Msamati

First published by Jacaranda Books Art Music Ltd,
London, in 2016
in *Speak Gigantular* by Irenosen Okojie
Copyright © 2016 Irenosen Okojie
Reproduced with permission of Jacaranda Books Art Music Ltd
through PLSclear (www.jacarandabooksartmusic.co.uk)

Gunk is a term in mereology for any whole whose parts all have further proper parts.

Get up. Try to hold your world. You can't. You let it slip. I know your world; car horns, aspiration, language, screaming traffic lights, spies. I see you. Your thick hair is overgrown, run an afro comb through it. Your wiry frame is still poised to move in sleep, to change shape at the edges of iodine-stained misfortunes. I showed you how to plant, how to sow seeds in concrete, yet your seeds don't grow. I demonstrated ways to sheathe knives in skin, yet you only injure yourself. Boy, you don't fly. You don't appreciate flight. You just want to prove what a waste of space you are.

Stop trembling in the fucking corner. Don't pick up that medicine. They numb you, sedate you, curtail your potential. Don't follow the script. You weren't designed for this.

It's a set-up. The system is fucking rigged. Your enemies plotted against you, danced on platforms in the sky, taunted you with disguises, reached into the chests of people you used to know. You rage because this city has broken you. This world has sucked your resolve through a pit. You rage because everything is a lie. Choice is an illusion. Its sibling conformity met you at the airport. Boy, you stepped into his fucking embrace proving what a waste of space you are. His smile made you forget your mother tongue while she battled the elements on your behalf, changing gears on any given day.

Remember Corrine? You told her coffee skin your secrets. She laughed, curved her wide mouth down to catch. You buried your face in her afro, travelled through it. You destroyed each other then came up for air. You watched her fly down the street engulfed in blue flames. A small universe spilled from her bag; notebook, pen, Vaseline, keys, items to trace on the scratched table when fear arrived with some creature's hind legs.

Your pity stinks. Stop cowering in the corner. Stop crawling naked on top of that wardrobe. You can't reinvent yourself from contained heights.

Darkness motivates men, mobilises armies. Use it. You are a warrior. Show me your roar. People are scared of your power, frightened of what you can do with it.

Once you wanted to be an engineer. Instead, those dreams drowned in the Thames. Instead, you walked off construction sites breathing sawdust. Instead, you avoided eye contact more so than usual. Instead, you resisted the urge to carry your internally bleeding head on public transport.

Follow my lead. Use those memories as lamps to see through your rooms. Nobody cares here. Footsteps on the stairs outside don't pause at this door. The carnival whistle hanging on the dented hallway wall waits for a cry that left you at birth to fill it. Your mobile phone stopped ringing. It's just you and me. You don't have any tricks. You just keep showing what a waste of space you are. You want to pick up that old taekwondo trophy and smash me to pieces. You can't. I gave you DNA.

These extras we programme ourselves to think are necessary – family, friends, jobs, love, companionship – these sentiments weakening us only serve as cushions to soften the inevitable blow. You'll die one day. Look around you, this is really it. Scraping pennies together so often it's become a pastime, rummaging for money inside the sofa. Cracks in the ceiling, the floor that's turned to quicksand. No cash to charge the electricity, your fridge door opening to reveal half a yoghurt, one-day-old kebab. This unending humiliation of you to yourself facilitates nothing.

The couple next door were once in love. Now, you hear plates smashing, arguments fuelled by alcohol, the ripping of each other's carcasses, their misguided notions of loyalty. You watch their ugly Bombay cat skulking outside trying to trace where it pissed over the remedy for doomed lovers rising through cold soil.

You sit by this window looking out, hoping for answers. Boy, I gave you answers. If you weren't so busy showing what a waste of space you are, you'd remember. Your enemies are everywhere. They want to destroy you with fear. Don't let them do it. Don't be a puppet. I taught you better. I showed you better. I schooled you better. Don't be a victim. This is what a victim looks like. This is what you look like. Don't look like that. Didn't I teach you how they operate? Didn't I tell you how you're conditioned? Don't swallow what they're shoving down your throat. It costs them nothing. Didn't I teach you about currencies that can't be seen with the naked eye? Yet there you go proving what a waste of space you are.

Are you a small country? Are you a fucking island? Don't let your enemies conquer you. Don't let them limit you. Don't let them gag you. Don't let them buy your cooperation with their sleight of hand. Didn't I give you ammunition? Didn't we sharpen our tools? Didn't we aim for our bullseye from every possible angle, every feasible position? Yet there you lay trying to show what a waste of space you are. Don't make me transform. Don't make me reconfigure.

I carried you.
I bled for you.
I suffered for you.
Stay close to me, listen. Every word I say to you is true.
Fuck governments.
Fuck systems.
Fuck everything that tells you if you're good you'll be valued.
Somebody always has to pay.
Make people pay.
We've paid enough.
Open your eyes. Get up from that bottom.
Son, this is the skin I'm leaving you with.
This is how to wear it comfortably.
This is how to camouflage when you need to.
This is how to start a war.
Remember: It's your world now.

Juno Dawson

Interviewed by Katherine Kotz
Editor   Ali White

Motherhood is something that is, obviously by its very definition it is gendered, and so obviously I've spent like the last six years talking a lot around gender, both in my writing and in sort of, my capacity as a mouth, as a gob, and it is something that is so closely tied to womanhood, that you could barely slip a Rizla between conversations on womanhood and conversations on motherhood. And so that's obviously something, that for me as a trans woman I've had these conversations before, and as well, I've been kind of confronted by them, in some ways as well, and so immediately I was intrigued and did want to be involved, because I think you can't talk about womanhood without at some point talking about motherhood. The conversations have to go together, and of course, as one of very few trans women with a profile in the United Kingdom, obviously motherhood has been on my mind, and womanhood is constantly on my mind.

But the other really striking thing is just the sheer question in and of itself: which is – I came out publicly when I was thirty-two years old – so in the first thirty-two years of my life, nobody had ever once asked me about children. It was just not a consideration. Nobody had ever asked me when, when people assumed I was a man, nobody ever once assumed, how do you balance work and life, how will you have children, will you have children, do you want children? These are questions that I was just not asked, when the world perceived me as a man. So that's how I know, without question, that motherhood is the domain of womanhood, because as soon as I publicly came out and said 'Actually, surprise! I'm a woman!' like the follow-up question after 'What's your name?' was 'Do you want kids?' And I was like, 'Well this is some bullshit.'

I don't think being a mum ever particularly appealed. The only brief window of vague interest I had in motherhood is when both Victoria Beckham and Melanie B were pregnant at the same time. And if like two-fifths of the Spice Girls were pregnant, I thought to myself 'maybe this is something I should be looking into'. And like, it really weirdly coincided with like my Year 9 sex-education module, when I was like fourteen. And so all at once, there was this kind of just – so at school we were taught, you know, 'when you have kids'. It wasn't really presented as 'if you have kids'. It was something to do (with) 'When you have kids this is how you will have kids, and it will be a man and a woman, and you will have sex in the missionary position, and then nine months later a baby will pop out.' Which is so hilariously limited, and of course, just one symptom of how LGBTQ people have just been failed for generations, when it has come to sex education at schools. I mean it was great that I knew how to put a condom on a cucumber, a helpful life skill if you intend to have sex with a cucumber, but now, it just didn't appeal. I knew I was a girl, I knew if I could wave a magic wand, I would be a girl in a heartbeat, I wouldn't even think twice. But when I role-played with toys, be that either Barbies, or He-Man figures, I always sort of created kind of like soap operas for them, I was much more interested in telling stories.

I think it's really sad when you do see people, especially fathers, telling their sons to put down dolls, because surely a father would want to nurture fathering or fatherhood. And then we wonder why we end up in this situation. You've got these men, kind of strapped to buildings, like the 'justice for dads' lot, or whatever they're called, kind of, sort of talking about how, oh my gosh, judges never give custody of kids to men, and I'm like, well yeah, because we have a society that has discouraged children, male children, from role-playing as fathers, whereas we actually encourage little girls to develop those kind of nurturing skills. And so I think it's a real shame, and certainly, I like to think that in this somewhat more enlightened age, that we are letting both little boys and little girls just play with whatever toys it is they want to play with, free from shaming and free from judgement.

So many of the conversations that I have around sort of feminism, all roads do seem to lead back to bodily autonomy, and that is that any woman should be free to make infinite choices about her own body, whether that is Botox and fillers, whether it is abortion, whether it is birth control, or the decision whether or not to have children. And there are still way too many women and girls in this world who do not have those choices. And I, for me, my decision to transition is a reflection of my bodily autonomy. I live in a part of the world where I was allowed to make those decisions about my life and make those decisions about my body, and I also believe in equality which is, I should have the same choices as a cisgender woman, and one of those choices would be to have children.

My good friends, Jake and Hannah Graf just had a baby with a surrogate, my friend Freddy McConnell gave birth to his own baby as a trans man. And that's because that was their choice. But that's not my choice, I'm really happy to be a mother to my chihuahua, and I suspect that is my lot. I am happy to be a dog mom and I think I will do that well into my silver years. I, like all women, reserve the right to change my mind. I don't know, and never, we must never say never. But I would be astonished if at the age of thirty-nine, all of a sudden, I was like, 'Surprise! I've decided I want a baby.' I just don't see it coming, and I think that's totally valid. I just think what I would like to see is we must somewhat move away from motherhood defining womanhood. And I think that's, I mean me and Germaine Greer don't agree on much, but that's one thing that we could definitely agree on, that the advent of the contraceptive pill has forever changed the destiny of women on this planet. Women are now able to have that bodily autonomy, they are able to control their fertility in a way that they were not, fifty, sixty years ago even, and that has meant that women have choices, and I think that choice, the decision on whether or not to be a mum, is available to all women, both cis and transgender, and the women that I think feminism should be fighting the hardest for, are those women in both this country and in other countries who aren't where we are yet in terms of this bodily autonomy.

Joelle Taylor

SLAMbassadors

1.

There was once a woman who gave birth to a thousand babies.
All night they poured from her like molasses
Congealing upward into children, each
With a simple hair-parting on the left-hand side,
Each smart and thoughtful, and each of them
With the potential of birthing a thousand mothers.
There was once a woman who gave birth to herself, and

There was once a woman whose heart was a dressing room
Whose womb was a stage
Who gave birth to a thousand children
Each body wrapped around an elastic O,
Bottle-fed on microphones, each baby an amphitheatre, a book.
There was once a woman who gave birth to a library
I have heard it said that all of her children remember
The maps of each other's hands.

2.

And perhaps you too will know
The cup of a boy's head bent in poetry,
The rhythm of hair and a palm and the smile he passes you
Folded into your top pocket,
Opened years later when needed
In a cluttered room that light had forgotten
East of everything else
Perhaps you too have children that do not belong to you
And it's time to pack their things now
To dig graves into chests
And to pass him a smile
That he can wear, in winter.

Siggi Mwasote

Nobody tells you! 'Oh it's a phase,' they say, 'Girls are complicated.'
I wasn't planning on being a single parent. I was in love, and I thought this was the beginning of me starting a beautiful family.

It started to go wrong at seven weeks. He'd moved into my flat and we were really happy. Then he wasn't. Then came the first wave. He threw me over a chair and locked me out – locked me out of my own flat. I didn't call the police. I didn't need to, he was gone by then. Then came three months of vomming and not being able to function without devouring the biggest egg-and-bacon sandwich with loads of ketchup, just the thought of it makes me want to barf now, but then! Nobody could have got in the way between me and my heart attack in a sandwich – and I needed this to grow a baby?

I knew I was having a girl. All of a sudden I started to wear pink – I never wore pink – and I started wearing dresses with flowers on, it was all very odd. Mind you, this is one of the dresses – I wore this when I was pregnant with my daughter nearly seventeen years ago.

I decided early on that she would be born at home. Hospitals are for sick people and I wasn't sick. I didn't like that bleachy smell either. How hard could it be to plop a baby out? Mummies had been doing it for ever!

My daughter woke me at 6.30 in the morning when she came into the world. 'Oh I don't think so,' I said to her. 'Far too early to be having babies! Back to sleep you go and wake me at a decent hour!' At 9.30 the adventure began – much more civilised. Birth was, well… Great. There was no screaming, no drama, the occasional sung contraction, 'Free and Beautiful' emanating from my stereo as she came into the world on a beautiful hot Wednesday afternoon with my neighbours applauding her arrival when they heard her cry.

My sister thought it was a really good idea to call him and let him know that she was in the world, still a very, very contentious issue. I was delirious with baby and in no fit state to make any decisions. He came over the next day and a few more times. Always when someone was there, after all, our last encounter was strangulation. Then I let my guard down as my bodyguards had better places to be so it was just the three of us. We played happy families for a bit, till the next wave. They've got actual terms for it now, coercive control, gaslighting, emotional abuse. Not then though, I was just a mad bitch who didn't know what I was talking about and didn't deserve her. He kept telling me he was going to take her. 'You better run,' he'd say.

He kept telling me that he was going to take her and I'd never see her again. He did a trial run. He made me pack a bag and he took her. For two days I cried constantly but I didn't call the police. I didn't want to scare her. He made me pick her up from a train station. That was the straw that broke the camel's back and two days later, after fifteen years of living in my flat, with my cat, my lovely neighbours and everything that I called home, I packed everything that was hers, my duvet, my microwave and the clothes on my back, a tenner in my pocket. I got my cat fostered and we moved city, just like that.

Over the next eight months nobody could know where we were. Our address was a PO Box number and my only form of contact was a mobile phone. But we were so well looked after, so well looked after, so well taken care of, and they thought it was hilarious that my little dolly of a girl, who knew all her animal noises, and could speak in sentences but just refused to walk. Fast-forward two days before her second birthday.
'Mummy?'
'Yes Angel Pie?' That was what I used to call her.
'I want to go to nursery.'
'Why? Why?' I pleaded.
'Because I want to have friends and I want to eat my lunch and I want to play.'
A huge rusty nail pierced my heart, I had to face the fact that she wanted her own world.

I remember being first in line to pick her up, seeing her beaming face as she ran towards me, all lunchbox and clothes and pictures, she just looked so happy, and I remember me, just stifling my tears of joy and relief. It didn't last though, that first-in-line business.

He found us. Threats to kill me and my girl. Why? I don't know. I still don't know. I did call the cops. They told me I should move. I refused. Not again, I've been through this once before. They did catch him and he did go to jail. I thought it was going to send me over the edge. But it didn't. Even having to give evidence in court – in front of a jury. He got a year. We haven't seen him since she was eight.

I've got all the books, I've read all the books. I lend them out now. I take lots of deep breaths. I count to ten. A lot. I walk out of rooms. I talk to my mummy gurus, professionals cos they've got grown-up children, and grandkids, and I do what they did. And I try, one day at a time. I wouldn't be without her though. All we've been through just melts when she laughs.

Athena Stevens

To love at all is to be vulnerable. Love anything and your heart will be wrung and possibly broken. If you want to make sure of keeping it intact you must give it to no one, not even an animal. Wrap it carefully round with hobbies and little luxuries; avoid all entanglements. Lock it up safe in the casket or coffin of your selfishness. But in that casket, safe, dark, motionless, airless, it will change. It will not be broken; it will become unbreakable, impenetrable, irredeemable. To love is to be vulnerable.

C. S. Lewis, *The Four Loves*

I've never thought of myself as filling the role of Mom.

Sister, absolutely. Fairy godmother, bring it on. Princess, yeah.

Let me put it another way: I thought I would be the President of the United States of America before I would be a mom. Part of this is that I was brought up on a weird combination of conservative talk radio and a church where, instead of earning badges for Girl Scouts, we memorised Bible verses. No sex outside of marriage, always stand up for the unborn child, and family comes first. I also knew that a woman didn't have to have children in order to be complete. And I also knew that if you did have them, raising your kids had to be your number-one priority from the moment of conception until, until... nobody ever had an end date. Having a kid meant your focus changed, forever.

I didn't see myself giving my life up that way.

I had, well still have really, a million books to write, injustices to fix, people to help and hear. Being a mom; I saw first hand how much of herself my mother gave up for me as a disabled child. A child for whom, even in the 1990s, she still had to fight for the right to an equal education. I got that education so

I could do the same for others, all over the world, not just the few children in my family.

These are all good, pragmatic, realistic reasons not to have children. Add to that the fact that I can't actually feed myself my own dinner thanks to a brain injury from my own birth, I mean it's all kind of understandable. Reasonable.

I used to pride myself on being reasonable. I figured it would be the only way to be successful as a woman. In a world that is waiting to call you 'shrill', 'aggressive' and 'overly emotional', 'reasonable' is about the highest compliment for which you can ask. Reasonable women get stuff done. Reasonable women might not have children, but they are still a force for good in this world.

Hillary Clinton is seen by many as a 'reasonable woman'.
Michelle Obama, a 'reasonable woman'.
And in the world in which I grew up, Phyllis Schlafly was a good, strong, 'reasonable woman'.

I've wanted to seem so 'reasonable' that my stock joke response is that my biological clock has been unplugged my whole life. If someone were to plug it back in, it would just start blinking '12 a.m.' Ha.
And then I remember that I am part of that *Oregon Trail* Generation: who had analogue childhoods and digital adult lives. Clocks don't flash 12 a.m. any more, they connect to a satellite instead.

As a little girl, people would ask if the doll I was holding was my 'baby'.

'No,' I would spit as if the question was absurd. I didn't give birth to a plastic doll. I wasn't a mother. She was my sister, or my friend, or someone who got run over by a truck and I was now very busy, night and day, nursing her back to health. Thank you very much.

My mother was always a bit concerned when it came to my flair for the dramatic.

I dampened that flair when I actively realised that, to get anywhere as a woman, I had to be 'reasonable'.

If you think about it – and forget everything you're supposed to say as an angelic, earth mother, model of modern femininity – if you were trying to persuade someone to buy a child, as a product, no one reasonable would buy it.

'Invest now in this thing that will wreck your sleep for the next… well, forty years as suddenly you become existentially worried about the state of humanity.
In the meantime, there's poo, spit, urine, vomit, tears: all yours to be unendingly mopped up day after day. Then watch as your hard-earned cash gets frittered away on every must-have Pokémon game. And just when you think you've hit your limit, they'll try to learn Frozen's *"Let It Go" on a recorder.*
You don't want to miss out: pick up your very own one-of-a-kind child today!'

I know my conservative, overly dogmatic upbringing was skewed in many ways but one thing I have seen clearer than many of my friends who have gotten pregnant: raising a child takes up time, and energy. Babies, kids, they don't slot into your timetable. Anyone who wants to be a parent but doesn't see that, isn't being reasonable.

But here's the kicker: life isn't reasonable.
Love, real love, the kind where you say the hard stuff because it needs to be said, isn't reasonable.
I'm not reasonable either. Nor do I want to be.

It was just after my thirtieth birthday that my friend Tim asked me if I wanted children. It's inevitable, you turn into a new decade and the jokes about biological clocks kick up a notch, so I knew just how to answer:

'No. I mean I don't think that's a good idea. My life is already complicated, Tim. Should I really be adding a baby to all this madness? That's just a bad idea.'

Tim turned to me, looked me square in the eye and said 'That's the first time I have ever heard you use your disability as a reason why you can't do anything.'

Our best friends are those who can see and then garner the courage to tell the truth when we do not want to hear it.

Now there's more to this story. Tim is in no way plugged into my biological clock but all credit needs to go to him in this regard: Was I saying I didn't want children because I actually didn't want them? Or was it because I didn't want to open myself up to having my own heart shattered into a million pieces when faced with the reality that, whilst motherhood was hard for some, it was potentially flat-out impossible for me?

Someone once told me, 'Having a child is like having your heart taken out of your chest and laid out in the open for the world to do with it what it will.' In my more honest and still moments I admit I already feel as though I bear the weight of the brokenness of this world more than most, simply because of the body I am in. I can only imagine my mother's perspective on the situation. Taking my heart out and opening it up for more pain? What reasonable person would agree to do that?

A few weeks later one of the most steadfast people on the team of folks who hold my life together left to go on maternity leave. From the second she told me she was pregnant she swore she'd be back to work but, to be honest, I didn't believe her. I mean, cut me some slack here, my friends all swore nothing would change while they were pregnant, only to find nothing didn't change with a new, small person living in their home. I'd heard it all before.

But she did come back. And yeah everything changed, her working hours shifted, and there was more focus to us working when she was in because her hours were limited. But at thirty-one, I was changing too. The way we worked together changed, but who she was didn't change. It was all very… reasonable.

A year later, she was still working with me: so much had changed within our company, within my work, that I was able to buy a home. I started looking at floor plans and calculated mortgages, all the while feeling very grown up, and then it hit me.
Whatever property I bought, I wanted it to be somewhere that I could have a child.
I wasn't seeing anyone, I was still popping the blister packs of birth control every night, there wasn't any immediate need to

plonk down the cash to have a spare room in the middle of London, but something in my gut wanted it. Deep down there was something that said, 'Buy a place to put down roots; you're going to be there for a while.' It was the early spring of 2017.

The flat was a good deal: the pound was down, the dollar was up, the new-build's location was exactly where London was making investments – parks, shopping areas, we are waiting for a Gail's Bakery to open any day. What I loved most about the property was the layout – the house gave me options for any way my life could go. Three bedrooms. One downstairs which was almost like its own unit with its own micro-kitchen, separated from the rest of the house, the person who helped me out at home could have their own space. Upstairs there were two bedrooms, one for me and… one for anything really. An office, a YouTube studio, a guest room, a room for a baby? I had found a flat that, no matter what direction my life went – marriage, baby, fostering children, career-driven woman who can't be bothered to meet anyone, taking in refugees, needing to accommodate an elderly parent – it didn't matter, this flat with its three bedrooms and two floors could accommodate any of the possibilities. During a time of my life when I thought I had the world figured out enough to dare to dream a little bit more about what my life could be, I bought a home that was not only what I wanted, but had space for a child in my life, should that day come too.

Three years later, in my perfectly Farrow & Ball-painted three-bedroom London home, I found myself with a two-year-old, who wasn't mine, during a pandemic and a national lockdown, for five months.

Her mother, a close friend of mine, had come to visit for a month during February, they extended their visit a little bit longer, only for it to become impossible for them to fly back to Lithuania when the lockdown was imposed.

When the time came to make a shopping list for a dystopian apocalyptic end of the world, I never expected diapers to be at the top. Or quinoa. Our two-year-old loves quinoa. I never knew a lack of quinoa in our cupboards could upset the delicate balance of world peace so much.

Turns out, I was right about a lot. Having a baby at home, even when she isn't 'yours', is a full-time job. I quickly learned that keeping a clear desk (or a smooth workflow) is impossible when a two-year-old thinks there's no reason to be so productive. Toilet training is in no way a straight line, and God help you if you put the milk in the red plastic cup and she thinks it should go in the blue. I had every utensil taken out of my kitchen drawer at least three times a week, and sneezed on because, well, pandemic.

And most of those plays I wanted to write while the world was stopped, never got touched.

But you know what I was wrong about? I can't do the whole 'running to the loo at the last second' thing, but I can teach a child to count in English. I love telling a little girl over and over how smart she is, because she needs to believe it now, before some prick wants her to believe otherwise. My flat has the perfect hallway to play Grandmother's Footsteps, and having a little girl in my home forces me to see, in full, the injustice we still expect women and girls to put up with.

I learned that it doesn't matter how much you try to shelter them, or how much their mother tries to keep it away, most little girls will find unicorns, and princesses, and tiaras, and glitter, and fall in love with all of it.

I also learned that even if they aren't yours, once you invest in a child, help them discover what they want and invest just a little bit of your soul into them, it really is like having your heart out in the bare open for the world to do with it whatever it will.

First person who breaks her heart, I'm going to fucking kill. That's a reasonable response, right?

I don't know if I'll ever be a mother. As much as I am happy not feeling that yearning and burden in me now, I know I could wake up tomorrow morning wanting nothing more in the world for no other reason than someone found the end to the cord of my biological clock. Or I could keep flying high in my own professional career and aspirations. Or maybe, just maybe, if you have the right resources around you, it is possible to do both, in a way no one else has done yet.

It is unreasonable to expect to love anything without it changing who we are at our core.

There is very little in this life that is 'reasonable', and so maybe it is unreasonable to expect ourselves to be.

Kalhan Barath

Director of Photography   Jay Rozanski
Music   Jake Strutt

When I was a child I decided I *never* wanted to have children.
The reasons, some could be healed – others couldn't. It was a
long time before I realised life shifted.

In one of those times that we don't talk about, but should,
I decided to go for alternative therapy; so I asked a friend if
I could borrow her nine-month-old. What I really needed to do
was to see the world through the alternative viewport of a
child's eyes. Why this child? Well fate or luck.

I tell you it was love before the day was out. That's between
Katherine and Zora, my puppy, not quite, who was seven
months older and so sure I had brought her a puppy of her very
own. Before long, we began to form a pack. Katherine began to
speak dog, and the two of them really began to teach me how to
grasp trust and love. Zora was attached, Katherine was attached,
and me, and I came to a point of realising I needed to look at
this whole thing in a future way, and how do I approach her
mum and say, Hey, I wanna look how I can, not just look from
week to week and month to month and what you need, and say,
I wanna make this years of what we need. That's Zora and me.

Terms and conditions re: Katherine. Zora – no impact on walks
or play. Katherine – only fall asleep on Zora. Continue lessons
on dog language. Mum – time commitments to be continued
and that they last until Katherine is at least twelve. Me –
commitment to Katherine, and that's what we, what was agreed.
Commitment till Katherine was twelve and I gave it.

One word, five letters and it changed everything. She said
'Mummy'. How could a two-year-old, how could a two-year-
old just change your life. I mean when I look back on that
moment today, I don't even begin to think, understand the level
of the gift she gave me. That gift is so important to me right
now, the love I know today is because of that gift, that day.

So alls I could do, because I didn't really understand, is reach out my hand and take a hold of hers, and the human dog pack way of saying 'I accept your way of seeing the world, of seeing us' while inside I was saying 'Heck! I've been adopted!'

Katherine, age four. By now we've set up traditions of our own. One of them is Katherine saying 'I don't wanna go.' But eventually Katherine flew a heck of a lot of nests. And Zora went on ahead, first, but she's waiting for me, one day, we'll run together. Sad still. Life continues.

Katherine and I still talk, we still meet up, we still visit, that's great, but there's times between that's lonely. But a friend, she had a bump and she offered to start the 'Adopt an Aunt' scheme.

Lemn Sissay MBE

Interviewed by Katherine Kotz
Editor Ali White

'For My Headstone'

Here is the death of the son you never had,
The hands you never touched
The face you never stroked
Here is the morning after
His bruises you never tended,
The laughter you never shared.
And here are the tears he'll never feel,
Your eyes he'll never see,
Whispers he'll never hear.
The apologies will squirm in his coffin
With the letters you never wrote.

See when I found my mum at twenty-one years of age – I was,
she was forty-two. She was twenty-one when she gave birth to
me. When I found her I hadn't realised that I was the same age,
a similar age within three or four years, as my father. In other
words, the last time my mother saw my father, was at my
conception, and her seeing me at twenty-one was the first time
she'd seen him since then. So what she experienced in seeing
me was a memory of something that happened before I was
born. But I wanted her to tell me, that memory, in detail, so that
I could understand how I was born. In other words I wanted to
go straight into my mother's trauma, straight into something
that happened to her which she has had to bury for twenty-one
years, and I wanted her to skilfully unload that baggage, so that
I could understand it. In other words, I was an attack on my
mother's psychology and my mother's well-being, and yet at
the same time, on a very fundamental level, she wanted to see
me and I wanted to see her. And this is why, most people who
find their birth parents come away from it eventually disgusted
by their own parents, because they're like, you know, 'She
wanted money, she wanted me to call her "Mum", she didn't

wanna talk to me, she wanted to keep me a secret, she wanted to, she wanted me to meet her round the corner and not at the house, she, she, she was frightened.' Yes of course she was all of those things, but you come back to her as a grown man to judge her, or a grown woman to judge her, to say to her she wasn't good enough, to be able to explain herself to you. You know it's the big mistake of children who become adults, who search for their birth parents, is that they think their birth parents should be answerable to them.

Now, number one, most parents don't think they should be answerable to their teenage children, period. That's just a given. And number two, it's so selfish to not have empathy. You see, you see, there is a lobby, against children in care, but against, firstly, the women who were pregnant without a husband, okay. In society, they were seen as a threat to society. So all the chips are against them. Most people will say, 'How could they give a child away?', you know. Even though my mother didn't give me away, even though I was stolen from her, the general narrative about women who put their children up for adoption, even though my mother didn't put me up for adoption, like I say I was stolen from her and I proved that, the women who put up their children for adoption are told by society that they are somehow evil or bad, or that they are somehow, you know, the phrase is, 'How could she give a lovely child like you away?', you know.

Now let's just take a really good strong look at that. A baby will always give you love. It doesn't matter what you do to it, you know, it doesn't matter how, you can abuse a baby and it will still give you love. That's a horrific thing to say, but this is the truth of the matter. You know, many of us have difficult relationships with our parents, but we want to love them, we wanted to as a child, even if they couldn't accept that love.

Right! When a mother gives her child away to be adopted it should be seen as the most heroic thing that a human being can do for another human being. Because what they are doing is they are giving that child away so that it can have a better life and one that they can't provide. What level of that is not heroic?

What level of that is not strong, what level of that is not the most powerful thing that a human being can do, is to give something away of its own flesh, so that it can have a better life.

So we have to ask ourselves, how does it, how does that not happen? There has to be an intervention so that that narrative cannot happen. You know, Moses did it, Moses was adopted, and he was, you know, sent through the rivers, wasn't he, through the reeds, you know. Of course, in truth, babies are not just left outside. They are left in places where people can actually deliberately find them, just pretend that they've not seen. Because this whole story is about pretending not to see, you see, so babies are left outside the Foundling Museum, you know, people say they have found them under a bush, they were brought on a stork, they were left near a police station. You know what, a lot of the time it's left perfectly timed for the other person to get it.

You see, this is all about narratives and stories, and guilt and shame. If we can convince those women that they're guilty and shameful, then we will, we could disassociate them from the heroic nature of what they've been through and what they are doing. And we can also cancel out the nine months of them having that child, you know. Now, so, we have to unpick a whole lot of, of very clever matriarchal, I don't like even the word, cos it's just overused but systems which are primarily there to dismantle a vulnerable woman, and also to disempower. I do think there's quite possibly, a thing that men have against pregnant women, because they can't control it, they can't, they can't do anything about, the, the, the new generation is being housed by the woman, and there's nothing the man can do about it, and I think there is a sort of, there is a sort of, a sort of male psychosis, that occurs quite possibly. I mean, I didn't go to university, I'm not a BA, but this is why men like my father, although I shouldn't speak about him, but yeah, I mean, he was married when he slept with my mum, you know. Yeah.

So the poem does not understand what I have learned, which is that I understand why my relationship with my birth mother is not easy for her. But the poem is very 'woe is me' you know,

'for my headstone'. I basically imagine that when I die, my
mum will then give me the tears, and she'll then be like, 'Ohh',
you know, do you know what I mean? But actually, what I've
learned about family, is that it's not true. You know, if you can
hold a resentment against your parents all your life, don't think
they're going to get to their deathbed and go 'I'm sorry… agh!'
The reason you're holding the resentment is so that you can
hold the resentment. Because whatever they did, they did a long
time ago. You can build a house on it, you can get married on it,
you can have a career on it, you can become famous on it, you
can get money on it, all on that resentment. The last thing that
most of us want to do is to forgive our parents in real terms
because that, that is the privilege of family. The privilege of
family is you don't have to forgive. And as somebody who's
never had a family in such a way, I… er, I sort of, I see that, I
see people take it to the grave, you know. Anyway this is called
'For My Headstone':

Here is the death of the son you never had,
The hands you never touched
The face you never stroked
Here is the morning after
His bruises you never tended,
The laughter you never shared.
And here are the tears he'll never feel,
Your eyes he'll never see,
Whispers he'll never hear.
The apologies will squirm in his coffin
With the letters you never wrote.

Actually I'd like to read another one for you quickly, cos, I
think that, even though I didn't have a parent or a family, I do
think that often that can really help you understand the nature of
family. And so, when I found my mum, she then left the country
she was in and went to another country, and it took me another
few years to find her again and then again, she did it again, and
then finally I found her in New York. She didn't mean to do…
anyway I'll just read this.

It's called 'Guilt':

Cold winds have frozen us
Walls of fear closed on us
The sky has fallen down on us
And fear it has frowned on us
The lightning has dumbfounded us
A dust cloud surrounded us
The rain it pours down on us
Pain has been found on us
Secrets they have bound us
Anointed and then crowned us
Whispers race around us
Fingers point down on us
Fists beat and pound on us
Our reflections astound us
Fear it compounds us
Defences surround us
Frustration hounds us
Guilt has found us.

'The Repossession: Lot 67'

A girl clasped by the sinews of vicious storms,
Of saliva spat through sanctimonious scorn,
Gossip gathers in teacups and tapping teaspoons
How dare a woman bear such waste in her womb,
They locked her in the watchtower for husbandless women
And counted her debt in the cells that were splitting,
Forced her to bathe by night in tin tubs of guilt
Or be damned to the suicide with the skeleton silt
They pressured her each day to study Mary Immaculate in
    pastel pictures
Made her eat the dead and dry daily bread of water and
    Scriptures,
And no sooner had the secrets of birth found her
Than the hospital curtains crept around her
No sooner had air swilled in virgin lungs and seeped through
    the critical mesh

Than they pumped and thumped their fists into her
And gripped their pound of flesh, bathed in blood
Without pressure, the womb weak and depressed
'Miss,' the bailiff growled, 'your child has been repossessed'.

The beauty of what's happened in my life is that I've been able
to, I've been able to, I've been able to find the documentary
evidence of what happened, and where the lies were. And I
don't think it actually matters to my birth mother at all, I think
she's been through enough, I don't think, it's like, it's another
country, she doesn't need somebody out there with a sword, you
know, 'I shall' you know, the shield, 'Ha ha… ' You know, this
is really, not, you know, this is, it's almost, it's almost
intergenerational virtue signalling, you know, because we do
that in families, we virtue signal when actually we're doing it
for ourselves. 'Oh no, Mother, I'm going to fight on your behalf
now!' And she's like, 'You know what, I've lived my entire life,
I get it, let it be.' 'Oh no, Mother, please don't, I am going to
save you your reputation, your this, that.' It's like, no, you
know. And we virtue signal our own parents, because we need
to find a place, a reason, a purpose of who we are, and what we
are, et cetera. So accepting that, I'm still happy to have written
those poems because I feel that they have enabled, empowered,
many others, you know, and that matters and also they've given
me purpose to live, you know.

Author Biographies

KALHAN BARATH was born in Ohio and moved to Leeds in 1981. She says, 'I'm probably not the best export from the US, but you're stuck with me now!' She was part of a housing co-op for years and loved being able to offer help to people when they needed it. Kalhan has found it very hard to be on the receiving end of help since becoming disabled and tries to give back to the community by listening to others and holding a space for them. She is a great cook and has tutored several young adults with learning difficulties on how to brush up their culinary skills. An unexpected joy of the last few years has been joining an LGBTQ group for fifties and older, which Kalhan never thought she would do. The group meet every week and have been a great source of support and solidarity for one another.

E. V. CROWE's writing for television includes *Pig Life* from *Snatches: Moments from 100 Years of Women's Lives* (BBC/BBC America), *Glue* (E4/Channel 4), *Coming Up: Big Girl* (Channel 4). Writing for the Royal Court includes *Shoe Lady*, *The Sewing Group*, *Hero*, *Kin*, *The Unknown* (The Site Programme), *Sex*, *Collaboration* (Open Court), *One Runs the Other Doesn't* (Elephant and Castle). Other theatre includes *Brenda* (HighTide/Yard); *I Can Hear You* (RSC); *Virgin* (nabokov/ Watford Palace); *Liar, Liar* (Unicorn); *Young Pretender* (nabokov/Edinburgh Festival Fringe); *Doris Day*, *A Just Act* (Clean Break/Soho). Dance includes *Live Feed/I'm Going to Show You* (Siobhan Davies Dance). Radio includes *How to Say Goodbye Properly*, *Cry Babies* (S1 and 2), *I Confess*, *Riot Days* (adaptation).

JUNO DAWSON is a best-selling novelist, screenwriter, journalist, and a columnist for *Attitude* magazine. Her writing has appeared in *Glamour*, *The Pool*, *Dazed* and the *Guardian*. She has appeared on *Pointless Celebrities*, BBC *Woman's Hour*,

Front Row, *ITV News*, *Channel 5 News*, *This Morning* and *Newsnight*. Juno's books include the global best-sellers *This Book is Gay* and *Clean*. She won the 2020 YA Book Prize for *Meat Market*. She also writes for television and has multiple shows in development, both in the UK and US. An occasional actress and model, Juno had a cameo in the BBC's *I May Destroy You* (2020) and was the face of Jecca Cosmetics Play Pots campaign. Juno grew up in West Yorkshire, writing imaginary episodes of *Doctor Who*. She later turned her talent to journalism, interviewing luminaries such as Steps and Atomic Kitten, before writing a weekly serial in a Brighton newspaper. Juno lives in Brighton. She is a part of the queer cabaret collective known as Club Silencio. In 2014, Juno became a School Role Model for the charity Stonewall.

SUHAYLA EL-BUSHRA writes for stage and screen. She was writer-in-residence at the National Theatre, where her adaptation of Nikolai Erdman's *The Suicide* was staged in the Lyttelton auditorium. Other stage work includes *Pigeons* (Royal Court, 2013, and tour), *Cuckoo* (Unicorn Theatre, 2014), *The Kilburn Passion* (Tricycle, 2014) and *Arabian Nights* (Royal Lyceum, Edinburgh, 2017). She is under commission with Kiln Theatre, Chichester Festival Theatre, the National Theatre and the Bridge Theatre. Screen credits include two series of Channel 4's *Ackley Bridge*, *Becoming Elizabeth* (The Forge/Starz Channel) and a short film for Film4.

JODI GRAY is a playwright and screenwriter. Plays include *Thrown* (Edinburgh Festival Fringe, Winner of Brighton Fringe Award for Excellence; VAULT Festival; Brighton Fringe); *Big Bad* (VAULT Festival, Winner of the Origins Award for Outstanding New Work; London Horror Festival at the Old Red Lion, London); *Peep* (Bewley's Theatre Café, Dublin; shortlisted for the Stewart Parker Trust Award); *Affection*, *hookup*, *You Could Move*, *Reach Out and Touch Me*, *The Front Room* and *SSA* (all Outbox Theatre, in London and on tour). She works with national and international theatre companies, including Vanner Collective and Living Record. She has also written the short films *Broken Meats* and *Sidetracked* (nominated for Best

Writer at Underwire Festival), and is working on the feature-film adaptation of *Big Bad* (dir. Freddie Hall).

HANNAH KHALIL's stage plays include *A Museum in Baghdad* (Royal Shakespeare Company), which marked the first play by a woman of Arab heritage on a main stage at the RSC, *The Censor, or how to put on a political play without getting fined or arrested* (Central School of Speech and Drama, London), *Interference* (National Theatre of Scotland) and the critically acclaimed *Scenes from 68* Years*, which was shortlisted for the James Tait Black Award (Arcola Theatre, London, 2016). *Scenes* has also been mounted in San Francisco and in Tunisia in a British Council-supported production. Further work includes *The Scar Test* (Soho Theatre, London) and *Plan D* (Tristan Bates Theatre, Meyer-Whitworth Award nominee). In 2020, Hannah adapted four Greek myths as part of *Myths and Adventures from Ancient Greece*, which were rendered as cardboard cut-out puppets online for Waterman Arts. She also adapted Ovid's *Penelope* as part of *15 Heroines* at the Jermyn Street Theatre. Her children's plays *Mrs Scrooge* and *Not the Gingerbread Man* were hosted by Fly High Stories online. Hannah's awards include the Arab British Centre's Award for Culture in 2017 and the prestigious Heimbold Chairship for Villanova University, Philadelphia, in 2021. She has been named a Creative Associate of the Samuel Beckett Archive, Reading University, for 2021/22.

KATHERINE KOTZ is an actor, writer and producer interested in artist-led collaborations with a social goal. Katherine is proud to be a Delivery Associate for the Coram Shakespeare Schools Foundation, a cultural education charity that empowers young people to grow in confidence and aspiration. Her acting credits include *The Motherhood Project* (Battersea Arts Centre), *Pop Music* (Paines Plough), *Happy to Help* (Park Theatre), *Elexion* (Theatre 503) and *A Pilgrim's Progress* (Yard Theatre).

MORGAN LLOYD MALCOLM was commissioned by Shakespeare's Globe to write *Emilia*, which became a sell-out success in summer 2018 and transferred to the Vaudeville

Theatre in the West End in 2019. It won three Olivier Awards in 2021, including Best Entertainment or Comedy Play. It has been optioned as a film and she is currently in development on this. Previous theatre includes *Belongings* and *The Wasp*. If the pandemic hadn't happened, Morgan would have had two plays produced during 2020: *Mum* for Francesca Moody Productions and *Typical Girls* for Clean Break. Both of which will hopefully be staged when it's possible again. She currently has theatre commissions from Headlong, Lyric Hammersmith and Clean Break. For television, Morgan is working with Merman, Gaumont and Moonage. She is also adapting her play *The Wasp* into a screenplay for Paradise City Films. She is represented by David Higham Associates and WME.

SIGGI MWASOTE has been singing for as long as she can remember. She has performed lead and backing vocals for various outfits over the years including backing vocals for Dave Stewart (Eurythmics). She has had her own jazz trio, a three-piece a cappella group, Just the 3 of Us, as well as lead vocals for Afro-Funk collective Lakuta, currently signed to Brighton label Tru Thoughts Records. Siggi's tours before the pandemic have included opening for legendary Incognito, Afrobeat royalty Seun Kuti, as well as headlining Love Supreme Festival and various gigs including the iconic Glastonbury Festival. Siggi's other passion is directing choirs. She has been directing both children and adult choirs for over a decade under the tutelage of Karen Gibson MBE and Mark De Lisser (The Dementia Choir). Her community choir, Spring into Soul, were finalists in BBC's *Songs of Praise* Gospel Choir of the Year in 2018. Siggi's proudest work to date is the raising of her seventeen-year-old daughter, Tulia. Heaven and Hell in the most beautiful, passionate, intelligent, relentless, fascinating package.

IRENOSEN OKOJIE is a Nigerian British writer. Her debut novel *Butterfly Fish* won a Betty Trask Award and was shortlisted for an Edinburgh International First Book Award. Her work has been featured in the *New York Times*, the *Observer*, the *Guardian*, the BBC and the *Huffington Post*, amongst other publications. Her short stories have been published internationally, including in *Salt's Best British Short Stories 2017* and *2020*, *Kwani?* and *The Year's Best Weird Fiction*. She was presented at the London Short Story Festival by Booker Prize-winning author Ben Okri as a dynamic talent, and featured in the *Evening Standard Magazine* as one of London's exciting new authors. Her short-story collection *Speak Gigantular*, published by Jacaranda Books, was shortlisted for the Edgehill Short Story Prize, the Jhalak Prize, the Saboteur Awards, and nominated for a Shirley Jackson Award. Her new collection of stories, *Nudibranch*, published by Little Brown's Dialogue Books, was longlisted for the Jhalak Prize. She is the winner of the 2020 AKO Caine Prize for Fiction for her story 'Grace Jones'. She is a fellow and Vice Chair of the Royal Society of Literature. *Web*: www.irenosenokojie.com, *Twitter*: @IrenosenOkojie

ANYA REISS began her writing career in theatre with her debut play, *Spur of the Moment*, at the Royal Court Theatre in 2010. She won the Most Promising Playwright Award at both the Critics' Circle and Evening Standard Awards that year, along with Best New Play at the TMAs. Her follow-up play, *The Acid Test*, was staged at the same venue the next year, and her National Theatre Connections play *Forty-Five Minutes* was in 2013. Her original version of *The Seagull*, directed by Russell Bolam, was staged in 2012 at Southwark Playhouse, and they worked on two further modern-day Chekhovs together at the same venue and then St James's Theatre. Since then, her version of *Spring Awakening* toured with Headlong, and an adaptation of *Oliver Twist* was at the Regent's Park Theatre in 2017. Anya has worked in television, as a core writer on *EastEnders* and a lead writer on Series One of Channel 4's *Ackley Bridge*. She is creator of Starz and The Forge's television production *Becoming Elizabeth*.

NAOMI SHELDON is an award-winning writer and actor from York. She studied English and Drama at Royal Holloway, and an MA in Writing, Directing and Performance at York, before training as an actor at LAMDA. Her debut play *Good Girl* had a critically acclaimed run at the Edinburgh Festival Fringe in

2017, followed by a transfer to VAULT Festival and then Trafalgar Studios, where it won Best Show in the Funny Women Awards and Best Show of the Week in 2018. Naomi was commissioned to write *Out of Your Mind* by BBC Radio 3 for their Summerhall live radio season in 2019. Her play *Vile Acts of Love* (developed whilst on the Soho Writer's Lab) was longlisted for the Verity Bargate Award and the Women's Playwriting Award, and was shortlisted for the Tony Craze Award 2020. She has various plays and TV shows in development. Naomi is co-creator and host of *The Pleasure Podcast*, a hit podcast about sex and intimacy. She is mother to twins Solly and Betty, and to her cat Lila.

LEMN SISSAY MBE Google the name 'Lemn Sissay' and all the returning hits will be about him because there is only one Lemn Sissay in the world. Lemn Sissay is a BAFTA-nominated award-winning writer, international poet, performer, playwright, artist and broadcaster. He has read on stage throughout the world, from the Library of Congress in the United States to the University of Addis Ababa, from Singapore to Sri Lanka, Bangalore to Dubai, from Bali to Greenland *and* Wigan Library. He was awarded an MBE for services to literature by the Queen of England. Along with Chimamanda Ngoze Adichie and Margaret Atwood he won a PEN Pinter Prize in 2019. He is Chancellor of the University of Manchester and an Honorary Doctor from the Universities of Huddersfield, Manchester, Kent and Brunei. He is Dr Dr Dr Dr Lemn Sissay. He was the first poet commissioned to write for the London Olympics and poet of the FA Cup.

ATHENA STEVENS is a writer, performer director and social activist. She is the Artistic Director of Aegis Productions Ltd, writer-in-residence at the Finborough Theatre, and Creative Council member and Associate Artist at Shakespeare's Globe Theatre. In 2019, she was nominated for an Olivier Award for Outstanding Achievement in an Affiliate Theatre for her play *Schism*. In 2021, Athena won the Offie Award for Best New Play for her play *Scrounger*. Athena is a Trustee for the Young Women's Trust, a Trustee for Theatre Deli, a Patron for Coram

Shakespeare Schools Foundation, an Advocate for Index On Censorship, founder of the Primadonna Literary Festival, a National Freelance Task Force member and a founding member of the Women's Equality Party. Born in Chicago, she now lives in London. Athena was born with athetoid cerebral palsy.

JOELLE TAYLOR is an award-winning poet, playwright and author who toured the world with her latest collection *Songs My Enemy Taught Me*. She is widely anthologised, the author of three full poetry collections and three plays, and is currently completing her debut book of short stories, *The Night Alphabet*, with support from the Arts Council. Her new poetry collection *C+NTO & Othered Poems* will be published in June 2021 by Westbourne Press. She founded SLAMbassadors, the UK's national youth slam championships, for the Poetry Society in 2001 and was its Artistic Director and National Coach until 2018. She has recently been commissioned to develop her spoken-word theatre show *Butterfly Fist* to tour throughout 2021/2022. Joelle is the host and co-curator of Out-Spoken, the UK's premier poetry and music club, currently resident at the Southbank Centre Purcell Room. A Radio 4 documentary featuring poems from *C+NTO* and presented by Joelle, *Butch*, was broadcast in May 2020. *Web*: www.joelletaylor.co.uk, *Twitter*: @jtaylortrash

www.nickhernbooks.co.uk

facebook.com/nickhernbooks

twitter.com/nickhernbooks